BASIL HOLDEN

# DEMOCRACY AND THE FOUNDING OF THE AMERICAN REGIME

Unveiling the Roots of American Governance (2024)

*Copyright © 2024 by Basil Holden*

*All rights reserved. No part of this publication may be reproduced, stored or transmitted in any form or by any means, electronic, mechanical, photocopying, recording, scanning, or otherwise without written permission from the publisher. It is illegal to copy this book, post it to a website, or distribute it by any other means without permission.*

*Basil Holden asserts the moral right to be identified as the author of this work.*

*First edition*

*This book was professionally typeset on Reedsy. Find out more at reedsy.com*

# Contents

| | | |
|---|---|---|
| 1 | Introduction | 1 |
| 2 | Reflections on the Revolution in France: Edmund Burke | 2 |
| 3 | Democracy in America: Alexis de Tocqueville | 18 |
| 4 | The Federalist Papers: Alexander Hamilton, James Madison,and... | 32 |
| 5 | The Anti-Federalists | 49 |
| 6 | Conclusion | 62 |

# 1

# Introduction

In the initial section, we not only clarified the essence of conservatism but also emphasized its universal nature, not exclusive to America. This holds true for contemporary liberalism as well, as it is not uniquely an American challenge to conservatism. Furthermore, it is not a recent phenomenon, tracing its roots back to the ancient Greek sophists.

Now, we turn our attention to four books that can enhance our comprehension of the American context, particularly exploring the interplay between conservatism, modern democracy, the American founding, and the national character. These include Edmund Burke's "Reflections on the Revolution in France," which serves to juxtapose the disastrous radical revolution with America's restoration of lost liberty. Additionally, we delve into Alexis de Tocqueville's "Democracy in America," along with the insights from Alexander Hamilton, James Madison, and John Jay in the Federalist Papers, as well as perspectives from The Anti-Federalists.

# 2

# Reflections on the Revolution in France: Edmund Burke

"In the annals of history, an extensive manuscript unfolds to offer us valuable lessons, extracting elements of prospective sagacity from the preceding mistakes and weaknesses of humanity."

## Burke: A Visionary Conservative Prophesying a New Era of Darkness

Edmund Burke emerged as the most insightful political figure of his era. Had his advice been heeded, the British government would have recognized that taxing the American colonists would inevitably lead to a disastrous rebellion. If his counsel had reached the French monarchy and nobility, he would have advocated for reform to avert the impending revolution.

Even in his own time, Burke presented a paradoxical figure - a staunch defender of monarchy yet a fervent critic of absolute power, even when wielded by a king; a devoted British patriot who condemned corruption and misgovernment in India; a devout Anglican who championed the rights of Irish Catholics; a self-declared Whig who became one of the foremost critics of liberalism, now regarded as a pioneer of modern conservatism. His reformist stance was consistently driven by the purpose of preserving tradition.

Born in Dublin on January 12, 1729, to Richard Burke, a lawyer and a member of the Anglican Church of Ireland, and Mary, a Roman Catholic, Burke was raised as an Anglican along with his three brothers, while his sister was brought up as a Catholic. Enrolling at Trinity College at the age of fifteen in 1744, he immersed himself in a broad range of subjects, displaying a keen political awareness. Burke sensed the impending catastrophe in Europe even as a young man, expressing in 1746, "We are on the verge of Darkness, and one push drives us in." Demonstrating both precocity and foresight, he authored a philosophical treatise on "Our Ideas of the Sublime and Beautiful" at the age of nineteen.

After graduating in 1748, Burke sought a career as a writer in London, balancing his father's desire for him to study law. Despite some legal studies, his primary passion remained in the world of letters. Burke's marriage to Jane Nugent in 1757 and the birth of their son, Richard, in 1758 marked significant personal milestones. He published the satire "A Vindication of Natural Society" in 1756, followed by the treatise on the Sublime and Beautiful a year later. Simultaneously, he worked on various historical projects, consistently advocating for an understanding of reality in its full complexity rather than simplifying it to fit abstract theoretical schemes.

Burke gained prominence in the literary world, albeit accompanied by financial struggles. Joining Samuel Johnson's literary club, he became the private secretary of William Gerard Hamilton, a member of Parliament and Chief Secretary of Ireland. In this role, Burke returned to Ireland, advocating for the rights of oppressed Irish Catholics under British law. His powerful criticisms led to accusations of being a secret Catholic, but Burke's motivations were rooted in his opposition to oppression and laws neglecting the traditions of the people.

After three years in Ireland, Burke returned to England as secretary to Lord Rockingham. In 1765, he was elected to the House of Commons, becoming the intellectual spokesman for the Rockingham Whigs, known for supporting reconciliation with America and guarding against monarchical influence in Parliament.

Burke, as a Whig, sought to defend the compromise of the Glorious Revolution of 1688, which limited monarchy by Parliament. He opposed King George III, perceiving ambitions for absolute monarchy. Simultaneously, he was a conservative Whig, vehemently criticizing self-serving Whig oligarchs and radical Enlightenment ideas illustrated by the turmoil in France.

Although often in opposition in Parliament due to his principled stands, Burke's greatness of mind and speech shone through when championing unpopular causes such as the American colonists, the native population of India, and the Catholics of Ireland. His most significant target became the French Revolution.

Burke's "Reflections on the Revolution in France" (1790) is considered the first great modern conservative masterpiece. Written with the spirit of Aristotle and the rhetorical power of Cicero, it served as a warning that the radicalism of the 1789 revolution was only a prelude to impending destruction. Recognized as a prophet, Burke accurately foretold the consequences of England's policies towards the American colonists and vividly predicted the French Revolution's descent into a blood-soaked chaos. Burke's prescience, akin to Winston Churchill's foresight regarding Bolshevism and the Nazis, resonates with those who have witnessed the devastating consequences of the twentieth century. The key to such prophetic insight, wherever it arises, lies in viewing events from the correct vantage point.

## The Conservative Perspective

It has frequently been claimed that Burke upheld tradition solely for the sake of tradition, appearing conservative only in his aversion to change and defense of established habits simply because they were familiar and established. However, such an interpretation fundamentally misunderstands Burke's stance. He championed tradition against innovation not merely for the sake of perpetuating the status quo, but because tradition embodies prudence — a practical wisdom grounded in the extensive experience of human nature.

In alignment with Aristotle, Burke rejected the liberal and radical notion that society is an artificial social contract, a belief popularized by figures like Jean-Jacques Rousseau during Burke's time and embraced by the radicals of the French Revolution. Contrary to such views, Burke emphatically declared, "Society is indeed a contract," but not a mere "partnership agreement in trade" or an arrangement based on abstract rights. Instead, he envisioned it as a partnership encompassing all fields of knowledge, art, virtues, and perfection. The ends of this partnership extend beyond current generations, binding the living with the dead and the unborn. Each state's contract, according to Burke, is a clause in the grand primeval contract of eternal society, uniting the lower and higher natures, connecting the visible and invisible worlds through an unbreakable oath governing all physical and moral aspects in their designated places.

This fundamentally Aristotelian concept, echoed by Chesterton and Voegelin, asserts that politics must be deeply rooted in the entirety of the human being—body and soul. It suggests that the proper order of human affairs mirrors the complete reality of the cosmos, ranging from the simplest material elements to the loftiest spiritual components. Acknowledging our given nature becomes the reliable standard for morality, with the acknowledgment of the Giver being entirely natural. According to Burke, all rational societies express their national homage to the institutor, author, and protector of civil society — recognizing God as the provider of both human nature and the means for its perfection, i.e., the state. In the vein of Aristotle's argument that we are political animals, society emerges as the fitting context for our perfection and happiness.

This perspective underscores the significance of specific traditions for Burke. Nations, states, or peoples are distinct entities with their unique conditions, histories, laws, traditions, customs, manners, and prejudices. If these elements endure over time, Burke reasoned, they must be grounded in human nature. The gravest mistake, as illustrated by the French revolutionaries, lies in condemning all ancient institutions, manners, and customs due to their imperfections and attempting to dismantle and reconstruct a society entirely from scratch.

## The Secular Transformation of the Philosophers

Burke characterizes the French Revolution as a "philosophic revolution," a satirical term pointing to the philosophes, radical Enlightenment secularists such as Voltaire and Diderot. These thinkers aimed to replace traditional society, particularly the Catholic Church, with a society solely grounded in reason. The revolutionaries' hostility toward traditional Christianity stemmed from their secular self-assurance, born out of the Enlightenment's belief that they possessed an exclusive understanding of truth.

According to Burke, the leaders of the legislative clubs and coffeehouses were intoxicated with their perceived wisdom, speaking with sovereign contempt for the rest of the world. The revolutionaries, driven by an Enlightenment Gnostic spirit, deemed Christianity a superstitious impediment to be overcome. However, they failed to recognize a fundamental lesson imparted by both pagans like Aristotle and Christians like St. Augustine: the core issue is wickedness or sin, not social classes, private property, technological prowess, or ignorance of sciences.

Burke emphasizes that history itself teaches that the world's miseries arise from pride, ambition, avarice, revenge, lust, sedition, hypocrisy, unbridled zeal, and disorderly appetites. These vices are ubiquitous, cutting across genders, times, races, social classes, and situations. Sin, therefore, constitutes the problem. While the effects of these vices can be understood and somewhat ameliorated, eradicating them would necessitate man's destruction due to the deeply ingrained stain of sin.

Contrary to this wisdom, the French revolutionaries arrogantly declared the establishment of a Republic of Virtue while acting with a viciousness that shocked the world. The ultimate source of this viciousness lay in their rejection of Christianity, sin, and the presumption that human effort alone could entirely cure the causes of human misery in history. The Enlightened thinkers believed that political corruption originated not in the soul but in unjust social institutions, orders, and particularly in a religion that espoused the doctrine of original sin. They sought to obliterate these elements and forcibly construct a purely "rational" secular order, anticipating the magical disappearance of past problems.

Yet, the rejection of sin alone does not explain the revolution's destructive inclination. Accompanying it was a spirit of profanation. Those who reject the sacred consider nothing sacred — not desecrated churches, guillotined priests and nuns, massacred women and children, nor property, tradition, customs, manners, or laws. In their eyes, nothing is holy, and everything can be destroyed for the revolutionary utopia. This spirit of profanation infused the populace with a "black and savage atrocity of mind," overriding common feelings of nature, morality, and religion. This bold spirit of profanation was believed to usher in a new, just social order.

However, instead of the envisioned utopia, the people witnessed Robespierre and the Reign of Terror (1793 to 1794), escalating social chaos, and ultimately, to restore order, the rise of the dictator Napoleon (1799). Burke accurately prophesied these events in his Reflections in 1790. His visionary insights stemmed from his respect for historical lessons and an understanding of human nature, grounded in Burke's conservatism. The French Revolution, far from being a historical relic, continues to manifest in the devastations of Marxism and persists in contemporary secular liberalism. Burke's prophecies remain relevant, with his analysis standing as painfully accurate — only the characters and countries have changed.

## The Intelligentsia's Preparatory Role in Revolution

Burke's analysis unveils a captivating but often overlooked facet: the intellectual and cultural groundwork for revolution orchestrated by the Enlightenment intelligentsia in the decades preceding the French Revolution. Burke notes that a literary cabal had systematically devised a plan to annihilate the Christian religion. Their fervent zeal resembled that of propagators of religious systems, driven by a fanatical proselytizing spirit.

Recognizing the pivotal role of controlling opinion, the radical Enlightenment intelligentsia strategically secured dominance over the key "medium of opinion" by establishing control over those who directed it. They methodically acquired control of avenues leading to literary acclaim, forming a literary monopoly. Simultaneously, they diligently worked to tarnish and discredit anyone opposing their faction.

A significant portion of their efforts involved rewriting history to depict the Christian religion as the sole source of oppression, priests as cunning hypocrites exploiting a superstitious population, and religion as the primary obstacle to social and scientific progress. The parallels between the philosophes who paved the way for the French Revolution and contemporary secular liberals are evident — media domination, politically correct reinterpretation of history, and a concerted effort to discredit traditional Christianity.

This approach includes delving into historical accounts, selectively highlighting instances of oppression and persecution by the clergy to justify their own persecutions and cruelties using illogical principles of retaliation. Once again, we confront the simplifications characteristic of revolutionaries. Their relentless quest to identify evil is confined to a specific class (excluding themselves), leading them to believe they have pinpointed the source of all evil. Convinced that eliminating this class would eradicate all evil, they justify any means necessary to achieve this end. In the case of the French Revolution, the identified enemies were the clergy and the nobility, and the revolutionary mindset sought the concentration of power in the right hands to eliminate what they deemed irredeemable classes.

# The Unraveling and Centralization of Power in Radical Democracy

The Reign of Terror, akin to the horrific atrocities orchestrated by figures like Hitler, Lenin, Stalin, Mao, and Pol Pot, is often misconstrued as a departure from the lofty ideals of the revolution, rather than, as Burke contends, a fulfillment of those very principles. The swift transformation of liberté, égalité, fraternité into the bloodthirsty tyranny of the Jacobins is attributed, in part, to Enlightenment propaganda that vilified the nobility and the Church while portraying secular rationalists and the common people as virtuous and good. Maximilien de Robespierre, a disciple of Rousseau, and the working-class radicals known as the sans-culottes, primed by propaganda, executed the terror by annihilating the nobles and the clergy.

However, the Reign of Terror wouldn't have materialized without the radical centralization of power by the revolutionaries. The revolution not only abolished the monarchy but also amalgamated the Three Estates of the French government—the First Estate (the clergy), the Second Estate (the nobility), and the Third Estate (ranging from wealthy bourgeoisie to workers)—into one entity. The Third Estate, absorbing all power and representation, was renamed the National Constituent Assembly on July 9, 1789. This consolidation resulted in what Aristotle termed "extreme democracy" or, as Burke puts it, a "pure democracy." Burke humorously recalls Aristotle's observation that a democracy shares notable similarities with a tyranny. He cautions that in such a democracy, the majority can inflict cruel oppressions upon the minority, especially when strong divisions prevail. The danger lies in an angry mob, fueled by radicals, capable of more significant damage than a single ruler, as nothing obstructs its unrestrained will.

In the hands of theorists unversed in practical politics, human nature, and basic economic principles, the radical democrats wielded power with impatience and supreme confidence. They disregarded historical arguments, dismissing the past as something to overcome, relying solely on the propaganda ingrained by their clique of historians. Their haste led to a fondness for expedient shortcuts, where the deficiencies in wisdom were compensated by an abundance of force. Lacking political sagacity, they became susceptible to charlatans, delivering themselves blindly to every visionary and opportunist. Consequently, having disregarded the counsel of experience and prudence, the radicals found themselves bewildered by the ensuing chaos when their cherished plans, fraught with evident but unexamined difficulties and defects, were put into action.

## "The Extensive Manipulation of Wealth through Revolutionary Economic Policies"

After successfully undermining the established order and wealth that had previously sustained the authority they now hold, the revolutionaries confront a significant dilemma. The revolution, accompanied by inevitable chaos and mismanagement, results in the collapse of industry and prompts those with financial means to conceal their wealth. However, the revolutionaries, requiring funds for their ambitious vision of a new social order, face the challenge of acquiring money. In their quest for a currency to revive their declining industry, they turn to an unconventional solution: the printing of paper money.

The choice to resort to printing money arises from the limited sources of income available to governments: taxation, confiscation, and the issuance of worthless paper currency. Initial revolutionary leaders seldom opt for taxation, fearing immediate hostility from the populace. In the case of the French Revolution, where the middle class and the poor, constituents of the Third Estate, were reluctant to bear the financial burden, an alternative solution emerged—confiscating Church lands.

The ease of this solution stems not only from the Church's inability to retaliate but also from the prior vilification of the Church by radical Enlightenment propaganda, rendering it susceptible to plunder. The ingenious plan involves seizing land and printing paper currency (known as assignats) representing the stolen property's value upon sale. Consequently, secular revolutionaries gain complete control of the Church, utilizing its wealth to finance their costly political agenda, resembling the early Bolsheviks.

Implementation of this plan requires some coercive measures, as the revolutionaries make their paper currency mandatory for all transactions. However, as honest and industrious individuals grow increasingly apprehensive, they hoard real wealth, such as gold and the products of their labor. Revolutionaries, typically lacking industrious habits, attempt to spend their way out of the crisis by printing more paper currency, widening the gap between promises and dwindling revenue.

The inherent problem, clear to those with a genuine understanding of economic and political history, lies in the fact that this "paper circulation" lacks a foundation in real deposited or engaged money. It represents neither gold nor silver, functioning as mere fiat currency—a piece of paper declared valuable by government decree. Burke cautions that madly printing such counterfeit money concentrates the remaining power, authority, and influence within the regime into the hands of those managing this paper circulation. Consequently, power shifts to speculators in land and money, unproductive and predatory groups controlling the government. These speculators, termed "new dealers" by Burke, lack loyalty to the regime, patriotism, or rootedness in the soil, caring solely for quick profits.

As the speculators amass wealth through speculation on ephemeral paper currency, the fundamentally sound pre-revolutionary economy transforms into a post-revolutionary gambling casino facilitated by the government. Burke emphasizes that the legislators have turned the nation into a realm of gamblers, diverting people's hopes and fears into the impulses, passions, and superstitions of those relying on chance.

The ensuing runaway inflation, caused by incessant money printing, fosters speculation, diverting people from productive labor towards short-term speculation to protect their assets from rapid devaluation. This situation benefits the few who conduct speculative machinations, while the majority, promised much by the revolution, lives in fear, uncertain of the value of their labor as printed paper depreciates rapidly. Burke criticizes the revolutionaries for forcing individuals into a speculative game they can hardly comprehend, with only a few able to exploit the knowledge.

By 1790, less than a year after the Assembly confiscated Church lands and introduced the paper assignat, Burke accurately predicts its impact, particularly on the common rural man. The policy creates uncertainty for peasants, who find the value of their money fluctuating unpredictably. This imbalance is likely to lead to resistance, mirroring the turmoil witnessed in Paris and St. Denis.

Ultimately, those controlling money without producing essential goods for sustenance end up coercing the real producers into providing them with necessities. The power promised to the people becomes a tool against them, as the ruling clique concentrates on preserving its newfound power and privileges. As Burke warns, France risks being governed by agitators and an ignoble oligarchy, built upon the destruction of the crown, the church, the nobility, and the people.

## "The Parisian Republic"

The economic turmoil triggered by the revolutionaries had a natural consequence: the consolidation of power in a select few within the city of Paris. This outcome, intricately tied to the principles of paper currency and confiscation, became a vital force guiding the entire legislative and executive government. Unlike the old regime, where power was dispersed across feudal divisions throughout France, the revolutionary changes centralized power in the capital.

The revolutionaries dismantled the former regional and local repositories of power, replacing them with neatly divided sections referred to as Departments—square areas measuring eighteen leagues by eighteen, further subdivided into geometrically precise Communes and Cantons. Although mathematically meticulous, these divisions disregarded the historical boundaries that had naturally evolved over centuries. The revolutionaries, driven by the belief that politics could be a scientific endeavor rooted in mathematics and physics, treated individuals as mere numbers or pieces on a squared political game board manipulated by technocrats in Paris. This approach starkly contrasts with a conservative understanding of human nature, natural law, and the idea that political structures should be built upon local loyalties, as expressed by Burke.

Burke emphasized that human attachments begin within families and extend to neighborhoods and provincial connections. These local affections, described as intermediate institutions, are precisely what the revolution undermines. Centralized power advances as local bonds erode, families disintegrate, and communities become increasingly reliant on distant governance, driven by either fear or financial dependence. The French Revolution, along with subsequent Marxist revolutions and contemporary liberalism, exhibits a consistent disdain for regional loyalties, local governance, church authority, and the integrity of families—anything standing between the individual and the state.

France, once a great kingdom, transformed into a scene of devastation. Burke's assessment underscores the rapid and comprehensive collapse of the finances and strength of a mighty nation. He quotes Cicero, asking how such a great republic was lost so swiftly—an inquiry that may echo in the questions our future generations pose to us."

# 3

# Democracy in America: Alexis de Tocqueville

"Materialism poses a perilous affliction to the human psyche across all societies, but its potential consequences are particularly alarming in a democratic populace..."

## Tocqueville: A Visionary Nobleman Assessing American Democracy

It is quite intriguing, to say the least, that a 25-year-old French aristocrat could spend only nine months in America during the early 1830s and produce what is considered, in Harvey Mansfield's words, "the best book ever written on democracy and the best book ever written on America." Alexis de Tocqueville's two volumes, "Democracy in America" (published in 1835 and 1840), stand as classic texts elucidating the strengths and weaknesses of the American character, revealing what we should anticipate and be wary of. Delving into the pages of

"Democracy in America" can be a startling yet enlightening experience.

Born into an ancient Norman family with ties to the village of Tocqueville, Alexis, born in 1805, was a product of the French Revolution that nearly jeopardized his existence. His parents were imprisoned as enemies of the state during the Reign of Terror in 1793 but were spared when Robespierre, the orchestrator of the Reign of Terror, met the guillotine himself in 1794. Witnessing the political upheavals of France, from Napoleon's reign to the Bourbon kings' restoration and subsequent revolutions, Alexis experienced the tumultuous events that shaped his understanding of governance.

Although Tocqueville witnessed the destructive side of popular government, he believed that democracy was an inevitable yet ambiguous force. In 1831, Alexis embarked on a journey to America with Gustave de Beaumont, ostensibly to study the American penal system but with the true intent of comprehending the essence of American democracy. His exploration aimed to unveil democracy's inclinations, character, prejudices, and passions, seeking insights to understand what to expect or fear from it.

In essence, within the pages of "Democracy in America," we encounter the interplay between the republican and democratic facets of popular government, vying to shape the American regime. While Tocqueville did not explicitly adopt Aristotle's distinction between good and bad forms of popular rule, he, like Aristotle, sought to identify distinct beliefs and characteristics of popular government, distinguishing its positive tendencies from its negative ones. In doing so, he provides us with a framework akin to Aristotle's, offering a means to evaluate our national character and the trajectory of our political system.

## The Essence of America (and the American Constitution)

Reading Tocqueville before delving into the Federalist and Anti-Federalist works written over four decades earlier, particularly during the Constitution's ratification debates, might seem unconventional from a historical perspective. However, Tocqueville himself outlined the rationale: to comprehend a nation, one must first grasp the "prejudices, habits, dominant passions" constituting the so-called national character, all rooted in a people's earliest experiences. To understand the written Constitution, one must first fathom the material from which the nation emerged—a deliberate and enlightening duplication.

The Americans were a distinct people, defined from the start by social equality and robust religious convictions. The initial settlers, religious refugees, came to a land devoid of titled nobility and political order, establishing a society of self-governing farmers. While Europe featured hereditary aristocratic estates, the vast, available American land rejected territorial aristocracy. The necessity for property owners' constant efforts resulted in small, independently cultivated estates, laying the groundwork for the enduring property-holding middle class rooted in agriculture.

Equally significant was the religious foundation, notably the potent Puritan influence in New England. If the French Revolution stemmed from Enlightenment skepticism, the American Revolution and its triumphs could be attributed to the specific Christian principles of the colonists. The Puritans, who identified as pilgrims, combined religious doctrine with democratic and republican theories. Their political egalitarianism mirrored theological egalitarianism, emphasizing the equality of all men before God. This view, rooted in the absolute moral authority of God as revealed through Scripture, fostered a distrust of monarchical or aristocratic government.

Tocqueville, displaying a conservative inclination, recognized these starting points as the solid and virtuous foundation of the American regime. Although he considered himself a liberal, viewing the promise and perils of popular rule with suspicion of privilege, Tocqueville did not align with contemporary liberalism. Like Burke and Chesterton, he was a liberal who embodied conservatism as we understand it today. He identified in the American character the elements that made the experiment successful: Christianity, self-reliance, and a longstanding tradition of self-government. Tocqueville emphasized that this character had shaped the Constitution, not the other way around—a crucial point for conservatives today. The Constitution's significance and efficacy hinge on the strengths of our character, as the failure of these strengths renders the Constitution a meaningless and ineffectual document.

## Local Empowerment: The Foundation of American Self-Government

In the United States, governance did not descend from a distant authority but sprouted organically from the grassroots. Rather than being a mere theoretical concept, self-government evolved as a practical necessity. It was not a theoretical starting point but an imperative reality for a people embarking on a new journey, initially tasked with the responsibility of self-rule. What Europeans debated theoretically regarding popular government, Americans urgently practiced due to their immediate needs. Positioned at the forefront of modern political theory, Americans gained an advantage over their European counterparts by grappling with practical challenges, as aptly observed by Tocqueville.

The fundamental principles that underpin modern constitutions, principles that were scarcely comprehended by many seventeenth-century Europeans and were still incomplete in Great Britain, found comprehensive establishment in the laws of New England. Concepts like public involvement in governance, tax voting, power agent accountability, individual freedom, and trial by jury were not just recognized but firmly established without debate.

The application and evolution of these generative principles in America exceeded the boldness of any European nation. This development was driven by America's unique circumstances, molding its political character. Without an established national government overhead, Americans were compelled to be political beings, shaping and refining their individual political nature through self-governance. Establishing their own government at the local level, these sturdy foundations remained conspicuous during Tocqueville's visit in the early 1830s.

Tocqueville acknowledged the importance of localism, strong family bonds, and the governance structures of townships, counties, and states as natural defenses against potential tyranny from above. He asserted that the strength of free peoples resided in the township, considering it the most natural governing unit, akin to Aristotle's village—a community of families that seemed to emanate directly from divine hands. In this setting, true popular sovereignty flourished, acting as the crucible for ordered liberty and providing a robust foundation for the broader society.

The inhabitants' attachment to their townships, driven by strength and independence, led to active participation in governance. In this localized sphere, individuals directed societal affairs, cultivating a sense of responsibility and a taste for order. The hands-on experience in township life nurtured an understanding of the intricate harmony of powers, fostering clear and practical ideas about their duties and rights.

Tocqueville underscored the organic growth of political life in America, highlighting a critical distinction in the manifestation of political power and freedom between Europe and America. While political existence in most European nations started in the higher echelons and gradually disseminated incompletely throughout society, America followed a reversed path. The township was organized before the county, the county before the state, and the state before the Union. This fundamental difference explains why, even in the twenty-first century, Europeans are more susceptible to top-down socialism, while Americans resist such centralized approaches.

## Ordered Freedom

As Americans constructed their societal framework from the grassroots, their conception of liberty starkly contrasts with the extreme democratic notion of unrestricted freedom. Instead, for Americans, liberty is an accomplishment, emerging from individuals mastering self-governance; in essence, genuine liberty is built on a firm moral foundation. It is not a matter of unrestrained freedom, and certainly not, as modern liberalism suggests, a pursuit of licentiousness. Tocqueville echoes the sentiments of John Winthrop approvingly in a speech excerpt:

"[…] nor would I have you to mistake in the point of your own liberty. There is a liberty of corrupt nature, which is affected both by men and beasts, to do what they list; and this liberty is inconsistent with authority, impatient of all restraint; by this liberty, Sumus Omnes Deteriores [we are all inferior]; 'tis the grand enemy of truth and peace, and all the ordinances of God are bent against it. But there is a civil, a moral, a federal liberty, which is the proper end and object of authority; it is a liberty for that only which is just and good; for this liberty you are to stand with the hazard of your very lives."

In this conservative perspective on liberty, Tocqueville emphasizes the conservation of our nature as rational beings, the elevation of our better nature above the realm of beasts, distinguishing us as moral entities. The religious underpinning of the moral order, far from being arbitrarily imposed, aligns with the "ordinances of God" to combat liberty defined as mere license, akin to acting as beasts or, in Aristotle's words, even worse than beasts since without virtue, man becomes the most unholy and savage of all animals.

Tocqueville underscores the intertwining of the "spirit of religion and the spirit of freedom" for Americans. Freedom perceives religion as its companion in struggles and triumphs, the cradle of its infancy, the divine source of its rights. Religion is regarded as the protector of mores, derived from the Latin word "mos," signifying habit or custom, with mores serving as the guarantee of laws and the assurance of its own longevity. The journey towards self-government commences with the moral governance of the self. Without it, ordered liberty degenerates into chaotic license, and robust republicanism descends into extreme democracy. Tocqueville issues a stern caution to Americans, urging them to be vigilant that their devotion to genuine liberty rooted in virtue remains unscathed by other, lesser affections, including the love of equality itself.

## The Affection for Freedom and the Zeal for Equality

While Tocqueville embraced American democracy, he was cognizant of the inherent dangers in the American fervor for equality, a passion that often precipitates extreme democracy, jeopardizing liberty. There exists a commendable and robust desire for equality that motivates individuals to aspire to strength and respect for all. This inclination aims to elevate the less powerful to the status of the influential. Yet, a corrupted form of this passion for equality lurks in the human heart, compelling the weak to pull the strong down to their level and prompting individuals to prefer equality in subjugation over inequality in freedom. Tocqueville clarifies that democratic societies do not inherently disdain freedom; rather, they possess an instinctive fondness for it. However, their enduring and fervent love is directed towards equality. They pursue freedom impulsively, making swift and earnest efforts, but if they fall short, they resign themselves. Yet, nothing can satiate them without equality, and they would rather face ruin than relinquish it.

Tocqueville aligns with Aristotle in asserting that extreme democracy tends towards tyranny, though in America, it tends to manifest as the tyranny of the majority. This tyranny doesn't impose itself externally; instead, it arises from an excessive devotion to equality, often termed "egalitarianism." According to Tocqueville, democratic societies possess a natural affinity for freedom, but their passion for equality is ardent, insatiable, eternal, and invincible. They desire equality within the framework of freedom, and if that proves elusive, they seek it even within the confines of slavery.

This relentless pursuit of egalitarianism can lead to the tyranny of relativism, wherein no way of life, religion, or morality can be deemed superior to another. The reluctance to differentiate between right and wrong, fearing evaluative hierarchies, is characteristic of extreme democracy. In this setting, where everyone does as they please, making value judgments is considered intolerant. Each individual becomes the arbiter of good and evil, ultimately resulting in self-deification. Tocqueville warns that pantheism becomes the natural religion of egalitarian democracy, as extreme egalitarians seek to encompass God and the universe within an all-encompassing unity. This self-divinization removes constraints on government, leading to the removal of any limits a person might impose on themselves. However, the abandonment of an objective moral order also paves the way for social chaos, necessitating the emergence of tyranny as the only remedy. Thus, an excessive passion for equality can precipitate the insanity of tyranny, but it is not the sole form of madness that Tocqueville cautions Americans against.

## The Insatiable Pursuit of Material Well-being

One peril facing American democracy, as identified by Tocqueville, is materialism, which extends even to matters of religion. In the 1830s, Tocqueville encountered evangelists preaching the gospel of prosperity, emphasizing earthly success over heavenly concerns. These preachers strived to connect religious beliefs with freedom and public order, often blurring the distinction between seeking eternal felicity and pursuing well-being in the present. This shift raises concerns about whether the primary objective of religion is spiritual salvation or worldly prosperity.

The American inclination towards materialism has deep roots. Settling in an untamed land, Americans prioritized their physical well-being. The promise of opportunity further fueled a focus on individual success and the accumulation of wealth. While this narrative holds positive aspects, a problem arises when individuals become excessively absorbed in practical matters, wealth production, and the acquisition of material possessions, leading to a soul defined solely by material pursuits. Tocqueville emphasizes that materialism is a perilous affliction for the human mind across nations, particularly concerning democratic societies. In democracies, the taste for material enjoyments is heightened, and if unchecked, it propels individuals to view everything through a materialistic lens, fostering an insatiable ardor for such pleasures.

The question arises: Does the purely materialistic individual attain happiness? Tocqueville suggests otherwise; such an individual becomes restless and agitated. As he astutely observed about Americans, their pursuit of happiness is marked by incessant labor. The unique American scenario, where anyone can rise or fall without rigid social classes, contributes to envy among the poor and anxiety among the rich. The nation's focus on meeting basic needs and providing small comforts aligns with the pursuit of material success, often equated with personal achievement. The challenge for Americans lies not in indulging in forbidden pleasures, as seen in aristocracies, but in losing their souls to the relentless pursuit of non-forbidden pleasures—larger homes, more comfortable furniture, and an expansive wardrobe.

Tocqueville cautions against the danger of Americans becoming mere consumers, toiling all week to indulge in trivial entertainments during the weekend. This lifestyle not only causes the soul to wither but also prompts rebellion. Materialism, unable to satisfy the soul, leads to a peculiar melancholy evident in democratic societies amid abundance, fostering a discontent that can result in a profound disdain for life. While suicide rates might be low due to religious prohibitions, Tocqueville notes an increased prevalence of madness among Americans, driven by the constant pursuit of material gratification.

Even if the pursuit of material gratification doesn't lead to madness, it induces restlessness and a fixation on unattained goods. Americans, in their pursuit of worldly possessions, attach themselves as if immortal and hastily chase after fleeting enjoyments. This worldly preoccupation directly contradicts the religious foundation crucial for sustaining self-government, eroding the connection to a transcendent moral order.

Tocqueville's foresight becomes evident in contemporary scenarios. The restlessness and social climbing contribute to a culture where individuals build dwellings only to sell them during construction, constantly shifting locations to fulfill changing desires. The phenomenon of house envy, as Tocqueville predicted, fuels the sentiment of envy in democratic hearts, propelling them upward in the housing market. The rampant consumerism and the credit gap, where individuals accumulate debt beyond their means, align with Tocqueville's characterization of the American character.

A warning from Tocqueville rings true: as our characteristic passions like egalitarian envy, impatience, and the desire for immediate material gratification intensify, they risk overpowering the prudent habits of the middle class. The peril lies in succumbing to unsustainable living standards, not only in personal debts but also in the soaring federal government debt. If Americans begin to perceive the government as the provider of all satisfactions, there is a genuine risk of surrendering liberties to an ever-expanding government, fueled by escalating taxes in an attempt to fulfill every want.

## Preserving the Essence of the American Constitution

The essence of conserving the American constitution—note the lowercase "c"—becomes apparent in recognizing it as more than a set of assertions on parchment. The true constitution encompasses the foundational elements and institutions that underpinned self-government: a social order originating from the family, a political order emerging from the town and township, and a moral responsibility rooted in the individual's relationship with God. True conservatism, therefore, strives not only to safeguard these original traits but also to revive them if they begin to decline. Interestingly, when conservatives advocate returning to the Constitution, they may not be reaching far enough. The Constitution, in isolation, is a collection of statements; however, when viewed as presupposing and safeguarding the traits and institutions that preceded it, it transforms into a masterpiece of political wisdom, serving as a guiding force for nurturing and sustaining self-government. With a deeper understanding of our national character, we can approach the discussions surrounding the adoption of our Constitution with a more discerning perspective.

# 4

# The Federalist Papers: Alexander Hamilton, James Madison, and John Jay

"When we delve into speculations regarding potential encroachments by the federal government, we plunge into an incomprehensible abyss, rendering ourselves impervious to reasoned discourse. Our focus should be exclusively on understanding the nature and scope of powers allocated to the federal and state governments as outlined in the constitution. Matters exceeding this domain should be entrusted to the wisdom and steadfastness of the people. It is optimistic to anticipate that, holding the scales themselves, they will consistently ensure the preservation of the constitutional balance between the general and state governments."

## Reviving the Significant Dispute

This chapter and the subsequent one delve into the arguments surrounding the ratification of the U.S. Constitution. Broadly categorized, the Federalists advocated for ratification, while the Anti-Federalists opposed it. However, this broad classification, though accurate, lacks depth. A more nuanced view reveals that the Federalists advocated for a robust national government, while the Anti-Federalists were wary, placing their confidence in state and local governance. Yet, portraying the debate as a strict either-or scenario oversimplifies the intricate nature of the Constitution discourse. The crux of the matter lies in recognizing that both sides sought a federal system of government, featuring a governing power representing the union of states alongside the autonomous governing powers of individual states within that union. The complexity arose from determining the structure.

The Federalists, driven by concerns about union dissolution, anarchy, and national weakness, proposed empowering the national government sufficiently to avert these pitfalls. Simultaneously, the Federalists harbored aspirations for America to emerge as a formidable nation, necessitating a robust and ambitious national government.

Conversely, the Anti-Federalists dreaded the tyranny and erosion of local liberty accompanying a potent centralized government. Their remedy involved ensuring that, while necessary, the national government didn't become overly formidable. Having fought a war for independence against the British crown, the Anti-Federalists were reluctant to surrender their local liberty to an overpowering and ambitious national government. Their vision differed, focusing not on national glory but on the freedom and independence of local communities and states.

Characterizing the Constitution, along with the Bill of Rights, as a manifestation of this tension between Federalists and Anti-Federalists is more accurate than declaring a clear victory for either side. It predominantly leans towards Federalist principles, favoring a stronger national government, albeit with safeguards. Unfortunately, these safeguards have, in some aspects, eroded over the past two centuries, especially in the last century, bolstering the federal government to a degree that might unsettle even the most dedicated Federalist. Present-day conservatives often find themselves echoing arguments reminiscent of the Anti-Federalists from over two centuries ago. A prudent conservative statesman must guide a return to the balance envisioned by the framers of the Constitution.

When reevaluating our founding, it's imperative not to overlook the historical context of the debate. The Latin root "constituere," meaning "to set up," sheds light on the term "Constitution" as the establishment of the government, specifically the federal government. Unlike the state governments, which had long been established, the impetus for a union of states emerged during the Revolutionary War (1775-1783), necessitating a united front against a common enemy. The need for a national government crystallized amid the exigencies of war.

The official establishment of the national governing body occurred with The Articles of Confederation and Perpetual Union, ratified in 1781. Despite the effective end of the war in 1783, it took merely half a dozen years for many, including the national congress, to recognize the inadequacy of the Articles of Confederation and advocate for reform. Instead of opting for a mere reform, the Philadelphia Convention of 1787 seized the opportunity to draft a new Constitution, driven by Federalists Alexander Hamilton and James Madison. This Constitution underwent ratification by the states, aided by The Federalist Papers, affirming its acceptance by New Hampshire in late June 1788. To allay Anti-Federalist concerns, the Bill of Rights, introduced in 1789, was ratified into the Constitution by the end of 1791. This concludes the historical narrative; let's now revisit the era when ratification was still a matter of debate.

## The Imperative for a Robust Federal Government (and Adequate Resources to Sustain It)

One of the clearest articulations of the Federalist stance comes from Alexander Hamilton in Federalist 33. Hamilton contends that the framers of the Constitution foresaw a significant peril to political well-being: the potential undermining of the union's foundations by state governments. Remarkably, during the Constitutional debates, the Federalists were apprehensive that potent state governments might overpower the fledgling federal authority representing the union. To avert the unraveling of the union and states going their separate ways, Hamilton emphasizes the need to fortify the union's substance and strength. The backdrop of Hamilton's statement is a discourse on the federal "power of taxation," identified as the "most important of the authorities proposed to be conferred upon the union."

Hamilton's stance is straightforward. Everyone acknowledges the necessity of a union, even the Anti-Federalists. This necessitates vesting certain specific powers in the national government. However, adhering to a "fundamental maxim of good sense and sound policy," Hamilton argues that every power should align with its objective. If the national government is tasked with defined responsibilities, it must possess the requisite means to fulfill them, with money being the paramount means. Money is depicted as the vital lifeblood of the body politic, sustaining life, motion, and essential functions. Consequently, Hamilton asserts that the "power of taxation" is the most crucial authority to be granted to the union.

Hamilton's plea for adequate funds for the union is understandable, considering the hardships faced during the Revolutionary War. The Continental Congress had to plead with individual states for funds, leading to embarrassingly depleted national treasuries. The Articles of Confederation failed to rectify this insufficiency. The Federalists, scarred by the experience of an insufficient federal government, were determined not to subject the general government to the tutelage of state governments again. They recognized the inconsistency of such a situation with the vigor and efficiency required by the national government.

The powers of the new Federal Government must be sufficient to fulfill its duties, and mandated power without adequate financial resources renders it lifeless. The national government cannot be in the position of begging from the states, a stark reality in 1787 towards the end of the war. Hamilton, in December of that year, bemoans the nation's almost last stage of humiliation due to debts owed to foreigners and citizens, with no satisfactory means of repayment. The lack of troops, treasury, and effective government leaves the country vulnerable.

To remedy this, Hamilton proposes allowing the national government to raise its own revenues through regular taxation methods rather than relying on voluntary contributions from the states. In essence, the national government must have the authority to directly tax individuals. Hamilton contends that no theoretical argument about government structure will bear fruit without providing essential funds to the national governing body.

## Determining the Limits of Federal Taxation Authority

At this juncture, Hamilton ventures into contentious terrain, particularly concerning the Anti-Federalists. Acknowledging the necessity of a national government and the impracticality of incessantly relying on states for financial support, Hamilton raises the question of what restrictions should be imposed on the federal power of taxation. He boldly asserts that "the federal government must, of necessity, be invested with an unqualified power of taxation in the ordinary modes." This, he contends, logically follows the principle that "the means ought to be proportioned to the end," asserting that, concerning taxation, there should be no limitations on a power designated to achieve an inherently limitless purpose.

While the claim of an unlimited federal power manifested

through unqualified taxation might seem audacious, Hamilton tempers this notion when considering the immediate context—national defense and safeguarding public peace against foreign or domestic threats. The unpredictability of potential military threats makes it challenging to foresee the required funds to address them adequately.

However, Hamilton extends the scope of the Federal Government's ends and, consequently, the necessary funds to sustain it. He contends that the Federal Government requires unlimited taxation power because the nation's wants are limitless. In response to Anti-Federalists advocating for a definite limit on federal taxation power, Hamilton questions the feasibility of determining a known point at which supplying government needs achieves public happiness. He argues that a government perpetually under-supplied and in need cannot fulfill its institutional purposes, provide security, promote prosperity, or maintain the commonwealth's reputation, energy, stability, dignity, credit, confidence, or respectability.

The primary concern for the Federalists is national defense, but Hamilton envisions a broader array of wants that leans toward a seemingly liberal perspective. Despite this, he recognizes the Constitution's role in maintaining a rightful balance of power between states and a limited federal government.

Hamilton dismisses concerns about setting up an overpowering federal government, asserting that the state governments are originally vested with complete sovereignty. Paradoxically, he suggests that the real concern lies with the continuing power of state governments due to their greater influence over the people. Hamilton, along with Madison, highlights the Constitution's clear delineation of powers between state and federal governments, emphasizing that anything beyond these limits should rely on the people's prudence and firmness to preserve the constitutional equilibrium.

The Federalists contend that the Constitution establishes these limits, emphasizing the people's responsibility to prevent federal government overreach. Hamilton warns that if the federal government exceeds its authority, the people, as its creators, must appeal to the standard they have established and take appropriate measures to rectify the constitutional injury. Federal encroachments would trigger a swift and determined reaction, with the states coordinating plans of resistance.

In essence, the Federalists argue that resistance to federal encroachments should not be challenging. The original national government's weakness, stemming from financial limitations, implies that weakening an overly strong federal government could be achieved by reducing the flow of tax money. Alternatively, maintaining minimal tax flow could force the federal government to limit its ambitions. However, the historical growth of the federal government suggests a more complex evolution that might necessitate a brief historical overview.

## Taxation Through the Ages: Wars, Speculations, and Perpetual Challenges

The necessity for a robust and well-funded federal government became evident to the Federalists during the Revolutionary War. Wars inherently bolster national authority, presenting a straightforward case for centralized control during emergencies, supported by the imperative need for taxes. However, history has shown that once the crisis subsides, the imposed taxes often persist, contributing to the expansion of government.

Before the twentieth century, the United States managed to evade this pattern. Preceding the Civil War, attempts at significant direct federal taxation were consistently rejected or promptly revoked. Excise taxes on items like tobacco, sugar, and distilled spirits, along with import taxes, served as the primary sources of federal revenue. The first federal income tax emerged with the Revenue Act of 1861 to fund the costly Civil War but was thankfully repealed in 1872. Subsequently, the federal government relied on excise taxes and tariffs. However, the passage of the Sixteenth Amendment in 1913 granted Congress the authority to tax income from all sources, leading to the immediate implementation of federal income taxes during World War I. This marked the commencement of a continuous expansion of federal income taxes. Despite tax reductions in the prosperous 1920s, levies were raised again in response to the economic hardships of the Great Depression.

The introduction of a new taxation method accompanied the

Social Security Act of 1935, solidifying a fundamental reliance on the federal government. Individuals dependent on federal power are less likely to resist its ambitious encroachments for expanded public welfare initiatives. World War II further augmented national authority, introducing "painless" income tax withholding for enhanced efficiency, diminishing public vigilance regarding the government's tax powers.

An alarming shift occurred as citizens began viewing themselves not merely as guardians of their liberty but as beneficiaries of government programs, including Social Security, Medicare, Medicaid, and others, necessitating increased taxation. Attempts were made to curb the escalating direct federal taxation, such as the Economic Recovery Tax Act of 1981 and Tax Reform Act of 1986 during the Reagan era. Subsequently, the Clinton administration increased taxes on higher income brackets, and the Bush administration aimed to restrict the tax flow. However, domestic fiscal policies and wars during the Bush administration led to substantial national debt, culminating in an economic crisis. The Obama administration capitalized on this crisis to justify extensive government spending and a rapid doubling of the money supply within a year.

The evident lesson is clear: the government's expanded taxation powers have facilitated its growth, a concept theoretically endorsed by Alexander Hamilton, though the specifics may not align with his practical justifications.

## The Federalist Vision for Expanding National Authority: Soft Despotism?

The truth is, the Federalist papers themselves presented a plan for enlarging federal power. It's crucial to understand the historical context. During the Revolution, state governments were firmly established and wielded more influence than the nascent federal government. The Federalists grappled with the challenge of how the federal government could acquire any power in such a scenario. To be precise, the Federalists believed their pursuit of a more robust central government contradicted human nature. Local affiliations take precedence because our affections, our love, inherently start locally—with family, town, and city. Both Hamilton and Madison argue that the development of a strong national government need not be a concern. Hamilton articulates this by stating,

"It is a known fact in human nature that its affections are commonly weak in proportion to the distance or diffusiveness of the object... Unless the force of that principle should be destroyed by a much better administration of the latter [emphasis added]."

This "unless" is crucial, indicating what might counteract the natural inclination to prioritize local over national interests. Hamilton even proposes a strategy to foster attachment to the national government: "The government of the union... must be able to address itself immediately to the hopes and fears of individuals, and to attract to its support those passions which have the strongest influence upon the human heart." This implies extending federal laws directly to individual citizens, embedding the federal government deeply into their lives, creating affection and dependence even at the expense of state and local authorities. Hamilton elaborates,

"[T]he more the operations of the national authority are intermingled in the ordinary exercise of government, the more the citizens are accustomed to meet with it in the common occurrences of their political life; the more it is familiarized to their sight and to their feelings… the greater will be the probability that it will conciliate the respect and attachment of the community."

He contends that by entering the spheres where human passions naturally flow, the national government would require less reliance on force, fostering strengthened bonds with citizens.

This insight aimed to allay Anti-Federalist fears that military force would be perpetually required to compel citizens to obey a distant national government over their local counterparts. Hamilton ingeniously suggests that increased individual dependence on the national government renders the need for force almost unnecessary. This concept resonates with the idea of the welfare state, which replaces local affections and natural ties with a national entity, overseeing familial and communal responsibilities. About fifty years later, Tocqueville coined the term "soft despotism" to describe this phenomenon—a milder yet extensive despotism that degrades individuals without overt torment. Tocqueville predicted that an immense governing power, focused on ensuring citizens' pleasures and controlling their fate, would gradually diminish the employment of free will, creating a nation of passive and industrious beings.

Hamilton might have recoiled at such an outcome, lacking Tocqueville's foresight. The Federalists believed the Constitution had ample safeguards against excessive federal power concentration, and they cautioned the people to remain vigilant. Context is vital; the Federalists sought to strengthen a weak federal government against robust state counterparts. Even in bolstering federal authority, the Federalists incorporated additional checks on federal power.

## Ambition must be made to counteract ambition.

Federalists took deliberate steps to introduce additional safeguards against federal power. Their mantra was, "Ambition must be made to counteract ambition." The Federalists aimed to mitigate the risk of centralized power by instigating internal conflict within the national government. The renowned separation of powers, distributing authority among the executive, legislative, and judicial branches, served as an ongoing restraint on any individual or faction attempting tyrannical dominance. Instead of creating a Constitution that consolidates power into a single entity, the Federalists, inspired by Montesquieu's ideas, strategically placed these powers in perpetual contention. This deliberate antagonism acted as a formidable defense, preventing a gradual concentration of powers within any specific department.

Recognizing the necessity for such mechanisms to control governmental abuses is, in a way, a reflection on human nature. Government itself is a reflection of the complexities of human behavior. If humans were angelic, no government would be needed; if angels governed, external and internal controls on government would be unnecessary. Crafting a government administered by humans over humans poses a great challenge: enabling government control over the governed while obliging it to control itself. While the primary control lies in the people's dependence, auxiliary precautions are deemed necessary through experience.

The Federalists, identifying the legislative branch as susceptible to power concentration, implemented additional checks within Congress. They divided the legislature into the House and the Senate, employing different modes of election and principles of action to minimize their interdependence. Rather than envisioning a wholly united, efficient federal government, the Federalists pictured the three branches as interconnected giants, constrained by tight ropes pulling at odd angles. The sacrifice of energy and efficiency was a deliberate trade-off, grounded in the conservative principle that human beings, inclined toward wickedness, could pose a danger when granted absolute power.

This ideological difference between conservatism and liberalism becomes evident. Liberals, focused on achieving significant good, embrace the necessity of great power. Dismissing the pervasive notion of human sin, they believe power can be wielded with unambiguous goodness. Consequently, liberals may resist federal checks and balances, opting for methods that sidestep these safeguards. Conservatives, recognizing the primary control of government's dependence on the people, value additional checks against federal tyranny embedded in the Constitution, such as staggered elections for Senators and Representatives.

However, procedural checks alone may prove insufficient. If human character lacks virtue, formal institutions and mechanisms cannot prevent the nation's self-destruction. The Federalists recognized the crucial role of virtue in maintaining a stable republic, leading to the next topic—the nature of the American Republic as perceived by the Federalists.

## The American Republic?

The American Republic is subject to a crucial distinction derived from Aristotle between good and bad political regimes, specifically a republic and a democracy. In this context, a republic embodies the rule of the many aimed at the true good dictated by virtue, while democracy entails the rule of the many focused on individual satisfactions. Although both Federalists and Anti-Federalists concurred on the need for America to be a republic, they diverged significantly on its interpretation.

Federalists advocated for a broader interpretation of a republic, tailored to accommodate a large nation comprising distinct sovereign states. Conversely, Anti-Federalists adhered to the traditional notion of a republic, asserting that a genuine republic, rooted in virtue and local affection, could only exist on a smaller scale. Their perspective held that the state represented the maximum limit for a republic, deeming the union a coalition of sovereign republics. Article IV, Section 4 of the Constitution accentuates this, emphasizing that the United States guarantees a Republican Form of Government to every state in the Union. For Anti-Federalists, once government exceeds a particular size, it inevitably becomes despotic to govern such a vast territory effectively.

Federalists comprehended the Anti-Federalist stance and responded by redefining the concept of a republic. Madison argued that the union was a confederacy founded on republican principles, necessitating a "superintending government" with the authority and power to defend against aristocratic or monarchical innovations. To prevent the emergence of an American aristocracy, the Constitution explicitly prohibited the granting of titles of nobility. The Federalists proposed a national republic overseeing individual state republics, each with its domain, where the national government tackles tasks beyond the capacity of state governments.

Despite the expansion and redefinition of "republic" to form an "extended republic," the national government's republic status remains intact. Madison distinguishes a republic from a democracy based on representation, clarifying that a republic, administered by representatives and agents, can cover a large region. The system of representation mitigates the impracticality of direct individual participation in government, facilitating self-government through elected representatives.

While both Anti-Federalists and Federalists had systems of representation, the distinction between a republic and a democracy hinged on their objectives—true good or private interest. Madison addresses the rule of the many for their self-interest as rule by faction, defining faction as citizens united against the rights or interests of others. The solution to control factions is not to abolish liberty but to manage its effects through a federal system of republican representation, ensuring that representatives prioritize the country's true interests over temporary or partial considerations.

The Federalist vision of a virtuous government faced opposition from the Anti-Federalists, who doubted the likelihood of national representative bodies containing virtuous individuals. They argued that the temptations of national power in the Constitution were inadequately checked, marking a critical point of contention in their ongoing debate.

# 5

# The Anti-Federalists

"Why did you reject British rule and declare independence? Was it a desire for constant change or to submit to new rulers? If those were your reasons, you now have the consequences in front of you. Go, withdraw into quiet obscurity, and accept the oppression willingly. Abandon the hopes you once had, believing that you and your descendants would enjoy the benefits of freedom…"

## The Anti-Federalists and Apprehensions of Federal Despotism

THE ANTI-FEDERALISTS REPRESENT A COMPILATION OF PUBLIC ESSAYS crafted by various opponents of the proposed Constitution. Similar to the Federalists, the Anti-Federalists commonly wrote using pseudonyms (such as Cato, Centinel, Federal Farmer, Brutus, Old Whig), but scholars have managed to unveil the true identities of most contributors.

Adding to these writings are the impassioned speeches of Patrick Henry, who fearlessly expressed his views under his real name. Anti-Federalist perspectives and arguments exhibit greater diversity than The Federalists, given that Hamilton, Madison, and Jay formed a small group aiming at the ratification of a single written document, while the Anti-Federalists responded from various locations, walks of life, and critical perspectives. Yet, within this diversity, we can identify common and compelling arguments against Federalist aspirations, the primary concern being that the proposed Constitution granted excessive power to the federal government, inevitably leading to the loss of liberty under national despotic rule.

Any contemporary conservative reading the Anti-Federalists cannot help but sense a profound kinship, and numerous conservative groups are emerging regularly, echoing many of the same apprehensions as the Anti-Federalists. In this resurgence, we witness a rekindling of the original debate surrounding the Constitution, but with a crucial distinction: everything the Anti-Federalists feared, and even more, has materialized. Fortunately, the new Anti-Federalists are not advocating for the dismantling of the Constitution itself, but rather a return to the original balance between federal and state government as outlined by the Constitution. More precisely, they emphasize (much like the original Anti-Federalists) the Bill of Rights as a safeguard against powers delegated to the federal government in the Constitution, particularly highlighting the Tenth Amendment, which ensures that 'The powers not delegated to the United States by the Constitution, nor prohibited by it to the States, are reserved to the States respectively, or to the people.

## The Significance of Intermediate Institutions as a Safeguard against Despotism

It is crucial to grasp the profound essence of emphasizing the Tenth Amendment and understand why Anti-Federalists were displeased with the absence of an explicit guarantee of states' rights in the proposed Constitution. All forms of tyranny, whether overt or subtle, arise from centralized power directly governing individuals. Centralization occurs by eradicating intermediate institutions—the family, local civic organizations, churches, clubs, and independent local governing authorities in municipalities and townships—that could hinder direct control over the people. Totalitarians seek absolute control and recognize that relinquishing control to smaller, intermediate organizations weakens their hold on the people. As Aristotle observed, tyrants maintain their iron rule by preventing communal gatherings, clubs, education, or any other activities fostering elevated thoughts and trust. Despots aim to eliminate individuals with lofty thoughts that question their power in light of a higher understanding of human nature. They also discourage citizens from trusting each other, as trust fosters friendship and courage, essential elements for resisting tyranny. Rebellion typically begins at the local level, where people engage in discussions about crucial matters. Tyrants ensure that leisurely discussions are prohibited, promoting ignorance among citizens and habituating them to have small thoughts, perpetuating a slave mentality.

Tyranny exists in both harsh and, as Tocqueville pointed out, soft forms. Historical records show that harsh tyrannies, like those perpetrated by the Soviets and Nazis, resulted from the top-down violent destruction of intermediate institutions existing below the national level. Tocqueville cautioned that an obsession with personal comfort and ease could lead societies to trade hard-earned liberty for dependence on the soft but pervasive despotism of a nanny state.

During his visit to America in the early 1830s, Tocqueville identified built-in safeguards against despotism, such as the family and the self-governing structures of towns, townships, counties, and state governments. America's historical development from the ground up provided a formidable defense against encroachments from higher powers. Tocqueville emphasized the township as the foundation of free peoples. American social order progresses from the township to the county and then the state, with each level supplementing rather than supplanting the lower orders, following the principle of subsidiarity. Despotism creeps in when larger, artificial authorities take control of areas that smaller, natural authorities should oversee. The greatest tyranny occurs when the national government usurps the self-governing activities of local government, extending its reach into the family's inner recesses. The Tenth Amendment guarantees subsidiarity, ensuring that the primary governing power of states prevails against the secondary and supplemental power of the federal government. The fundamental principle is simple: more general, complex, and remote power should not infringe upon what more particular, simpler, and local power can handle. This is the only way to preserve liberty against despotic encroachments by the federal government, explaining the Anti-Federalists' dissatisfaction with the proposed Constitution's lack of an explicit guarantee of state sovereignty.

The liberty championed by the Anti-Federalists is not democratic liberty—freedom to do whatever one wants—but the freedom of citizens in a republic to engage in self-government on the most natural levels. This self-governing activity trains citizens from the ground up in practices that produce ordered liberty and cultivates the virtues necessary for true self-rule. When the Anti-Federalists defended states as republics, they envisioned preserving this self-governing activity threatened by the development of a strong national government.

Therefore, the Anti-Federalists resisted the ratification of the Constitution. Cato, representing New York Governor George Clinton, contended that the members of the Philadelphia Constitutional Convention exceeded their authority by presenting a new political structure to Congress. According to Cato, this structure consolidated the states into one government, deviating from the confederated league established under the Articles of Confederation. The Anti-Federalists believed that an empowered national government would destroy state republics and supplant the layers of ordered liberty they nurtured and protected. They argued that a union on such a large scale could only be despotic and unnatural, working against the real, natural, and original sources of social union. The strongest principle of union, according to the Anti-Federalists, resides within domestic walls, with ties of the parent exceeding all others. As individuals depart from home, the next general principle of union is among citizens of the same state, where acquaintance, habits, and fortunes foster affection and attachment. The state, being the natural limit of a republic, is large enough to provide everything needed and desired but small enough to be knowledgeable about and directly concerned with the particular conditions of its citizens. The Anti-Federalists, particularly Federal Farmer (Melancton Smith), suggested that those opposing the Constitution should be labeled 'republicans,' while the Federalists were more appropriately termed 'anti-republicans.'

Although the Constitution significantly strengthened the federal government, the Anti-Federalists believed it lacked adequate safeguards against federal despotism. In the words of Centinel, believed to be Samuel Bryan, a Pennsylvanian Anti-Federalist, 'The general government would necessarily annihilate the particular governments,' especially through its power of taxation. This would supersede and destroy the security of personal rights provided by state constitutions, necessitating the inclusion of a bill of rights in the new federal government plan.

## The Menacing Authority of Taxation and the Incursion of Federal Bureaucracy

As explored in the preceding chapter, the Federalists conceded that bolstering federal taxation was indispensable to provide the energy they believed the government required. Unsurprisingly, the Anti-Federalists concurred but were discontented about granting such authority. Centinel, a prominent Anti-Federalist, criticized the Federalist argument, asserting that they exploit a "crisis," capitalizing on the nation's "temporary and extraordinary difficulties" caused by prolonged war to establish enduring additional powers. The power to tax for the "common defence" is distinguishable from the claimed constitutional power of the federal government to levy taxes for the "general welfare," a phrase so comprehensive that it encompasses every form of taxation, both external and internal. According to Centinel, this broad interpretation would grant the federal government boundless taxing powers, as whoever controls the purse strings possesses complete dominion.

To appreciate the Anti-Federalists' foresighted concerns about granting internal taxing powers to the new federal government, one need only consider the Internal Revenue Service (IRS), founded by Abraham Lincoln in 1862 under the name "Bureau of Internal Revenue" to oversee the collection of the country's inaugural Income Tax. An examination of the expansion of government taxation and spending since the inception of programs like Social Security, Medicare, and Medicaid reinforces the apprehensions expressed by the Anti-Federalists. These entitlement programs now consume a substantial portion of the federal budget.

Luther Martin, an Anti-Federalist, vividly warned that unlimited taxing power would enable the federal government to exploit the people endlessly without control or restraint. He argued that the primary power of internal taxation should remain with the states, as they are better equipped to assess their citizens' circumstances and determine the most convenient and efficient means of collecting funds. Another Anti-Federalist,

Brutus (Robert Yates), humorously and accurately depicted the intrusive nature of unlimited taxation into every aspect of individuals' lives. He envisioned this power penetrating every corner of cities and the countryside, affecting people in their daily activities, even accompanying them to social events, monitoring their domestic affairs, and persistently demanding, "GIVE! GIVE!"

The issue is not merely about additional taxes but rather about expanding government. Granting unlimited taxing powers to the federal government will result in an unrestricted federal government. Federal Farmer, an insightful Anti-Federalist, noted that external taxes alone, such as import duties, would be insufficient for the Federalists' desire for a more comprehensive national government. The larger it becomes, the more it will create laws and officers to support its expansion, requiring a constant increase in funding. This will lead to the activation of internal taxation, involving federal assessors and collectors spread across the vast country. Consequently, a permanent system of tax laws executed by federal officers within the states will emerge.

The relentless growth of the federal government will give rise to an expansive and invasive federal bureaucracy. This top-down tyranny will become increasingly oppressive, with the federal government prioritizing self-preservation and expansion over public good. Federal Farmer warned of the dangers of a large standing army, emphasizing the equally detrimental impact of a vast number of self-serving, unprincipled civil officers. Given the country's size, numerous officers will be necessary to execute a national system, turning them into direct dependents on Congress. Consequently, the welfare of this bureaucratic class will become a primary goal for the national legislature.

To prevent limitless growth, the Anti-Federalists proposed establishing a "federal republic" or a "confederation" of state republics, where each state expressly retains its sovereignty, and powers not given to Congress are preserved. In this federal republic, state governments must serve as barriers between Congress and the people's pockets, opposing heavy internal taxes and oppressive measures. The Anti-Federalists argue that endless federal bureaucracies cannot thrive without feeding on tax dollars.

The proposed Constitution, lacking a Bill of Rights, fails to provide protection against this limitless growth. In the event that the national Congress imposes unnecessary and oppressive taxes, the Constitution offers no remedies, leaving the people with no option but to endure or resort to resistance, a last resort founded in self-defense.

However, Tocqueville reminds us of a neglected means of resistance and defense: self-control. If we rely on the federal government for comprehensive welfare, bailouts, subsidies, and endless funding for various endeavors, we must also shoulder the blame when we succumb to the soft despotism it offers. Without the virtue of self-control, why should we expect the federal government to exercise restraint?"

## Other Alarming Authorities of Congress and the Supreme Court

The Anti-Federalists were not solely concerned about the proposed federal taxing authority. As outlined earlier, they were deeply troubled by the potential consequences of the federal government taking on the vague responsibility of promoting the "general welfare." Their apprehension escalated due to two constitutional assertions: firstly, that Congress had the power "To make all Laws which shall be necessary and proper for carrying into Execution the foregoing Powers, and all other Powers vested by this Constitution in the Government of the United States, or in any Department thereof,"22 and secondly, that "the Constitution... shall be the supreme Law of the Land; and the Judges in every State shall be bound thereby, any Thing in the constitution or Laws of any State to the Contrary notwithstanding."23 The first provision grants boundless power to Congress, while the second endows unlimited power upon the federal judiciary, primarily the Supreme Court. Coupled with the authority of direct, internal taxation, these provisions would lead to an absolute concentration of power at the federal level,24 echoing Brutus's assertion that "there is [then] nothing valuable to human nature, nothing dear to freemen, but what is within its power."25 Patrick Henry cautioned that this Constitution could override and suspend any state laws conflicting with its oppressive operation, utilizing the power of direct taxation, which suspends state Bill of Rights. The Constitution explicitly states that Congress can make laws necessary to execute its powers, surpassing state laws and constitutions.

Regarding the "necessary and proper" clause, the danger arises from the Constitution's ambiguity and human nature. Brutus emphasized the central issue of granting Congress extensive powers to promote the general welfare: a concept so vague that nearly anyone can manipulate it for any purpose.

"It will then be [a] matter of opinion, what tends to the general welfare; and the Congress will be the only judges in the matter. To provide for the general welfare is an abstract proposition, which mankind differ in the explanation of, as much as they do on any political or moral proposition that can be proposed; the most opposite measures may be pursued by different parties, and both may profess that they have in view the general welfare; and both sides may be honest in their professions, or both may have sinister views."[27]

If Congress can utilize it for anything, they undoubtedly will. The proposed federal powers will be exacerbated by the natural inclination of "every man, and every body of men" who, "invested with power, are ever disposed to increase it, and to acquire a superiority over everything that stands in their way."[28]

As for the Supreme Court, Brutus pointed out that the Constitution declares itself the supreme law of the land. Its Preamble asserts that the supreme law aims to "form a more perfect Union, establish Justice, insure domestic Tranquility, provide for the common defence, promote the general Welfare, and secure the Blessings of Liberty to ourselves and our Posterity." The very vagueness of these goals implies that the federal judiciary must "explain the constitution, not only according to its letter, but according to its spirit and intention." No one doubts that they "would strongly incline to give it such a construction as to extend the powers of the general government."29 The Supreme Court's power to decide upon the Constitution's meaning, according to its spirit and intention, means it is not subordinate to but above the legislature. While it doesn't directly make laws, it establishes judicial principles of interpretation, enlarging the legislature's power beyond all bounds. The power of the Supreme Court and Congress grows simultaneously, and "in proportion as the general government acquires power and jurisdiction, by the liberal construction which the judges may give the constitution, will those of the states lose its rights until they become so trifling and unimportant as not to be worth having."32

Emphasizing the term "liberal" in this context, Brutus does not refer to the modern sense of the term related to the far Left. Instead, he means that the Supreme Court will inevitably tend to expand federal power through broad interpretations of the Constitution. There is a significant connection between this warning and the advancement of liberal causes through judicial activism.

Liberalism, seeking centralized power, especially through the judiciary, acts as a revolutionary force attempting to change, from the top-down, the habits, beliefs, customs, and institutions at the local level. Liberalism, a top-down secular revolution, aims to transform a conservative culture built on Judeo-Christian beliefs from the bottom up. For them, promoting the general welfare involves changing conservative views on marriage, family, sexuality, abortion, and euthanasia, which still largely define the "locals" clinging to their "guns and religion," as contemptuously mentioned by Obama.

As the "locals" still have voting power, staging a cultural revolution through Congress proves challenging. However, staging a revolution through the Supreme Court and the federal court system is more feasible. Winning a single case, such as Roe v. Wade, can overturn state laws, moral convictions, and arguments to the contrary. This allows Congress to advance the agenda with more extensive laws based on the original judicial victory. This was exactly the fear of Brutus: court cases establish principles and precedents that strike down state and local laws, giving Congress the power to enact legislation that promotes the revolution.

Having the unlimited ability to define the Constitution and strike down any laws, even those made by Congress, as unconstitutional means, for Brutus, that there "is no power above them [the Supreme Court], to control… their decisions… they cannot be controlled by the laws of the legislature. In short, they are independent of the people, of the legislature, and of every power under heaven. Men placed in this situation will generally soon feel themselves independent of heaven itself."33 This may explain why they feel entirely free to interpret the First Amendment, stating that "Congress shall make no law respecting the establishment of religion," to mean that religion must be eradicated from the public square.

# 6

# Conclusion

AS I MENTIONED FROM THE OUTSET, THERE EXISTS A PLETHORA OF books that every conservative should delve into, and the list goes on. The supply of books, both commendable and dubious, seems endless, with the latter often overshadowing the former. Consequently, I could readily compile Ten More Books Every Conservative Must Read, and with even greater ease, Ten More Books that Adversely Impacted the World.

However, I trust that readers, having reached the conclusion, will concur that the fourteen books I've singled out as essential reads can enrich conservative discourse, elevating us beyond the superficiality of our social media-driven era to rediscover the wisdom rooted in experience.

The quintessential guide for conservatives isn't a tome but the lessons drawn from nature and human nature, accessible to all. This explains why practical wisdom—and inherent conservatism—are frequently found among ordinary people, especially rural dwellers immersed in the natural rhythms, agricultural pursuits, and tight-knit bonds of family and community. In contrast, urban intellectuals, considering themselves exceptionally clever, often lack such practical wisdom. Conservatives advocate for local governance by local individuals precisely because they believe that ordinary people are wellsprings of practical wisdom.

Nevertheless, the tradition of consolidating practical wisdom into a book is both ancient and commendable. Examples include the Proverbs of the Old Testament. The term "old" holds significance here, countering the modern bias that equates old with outdated and foolish. This bias disconnects us from the wisdom and experience that could navigate us through contemporary challenges. Rather than benefitting from the lessons of the past, we resemble children oblivious to the insights that history offers for present guidance. Compounding this, our disregard for the past breeds foolishness, while our increasing technological prowess makes us more powerful. However, power in the hands of a fool is evidently perilous. For our survival, as technological advancements burgeon, our conservatism must intensify—binding us to ancient insights about human nature, particularly regarding pride, folly, sin, and the imperative of restraining power.

The conservative apprehension of big government stems from its tendency to centralize power, placing immense authority in the hands of a select few who, when wielding such power, magnify their personal characteristics—pride, folly, and sin. If humans were consistently wise, prudent, and virtuous, concentration of political power wouldn't elicit fear.

Another crucial consideration is that conservatives value differences and specificities, unlike liberals who dismiss them. Liberals advocate for universal liberalism as the culmination of history, leading to a homogenized world culture. To liberals, anti-federalist ideas that decentralize power to specific communities are unappealing. Liberals favor entities like the United Nations but are averse to actual nations.

Liberalism exhibits inherent animosity toward genuine religion while remaining amicable toward vague spirituality. Vague spirituality, lacking definable content, can be co-opted by liberalism. In contrast, deeply rooted beliefs of specific communities spanning centuries obstruct liberalism's progress toward a homogenized, secular global culture. Christianity, in particular, poses the greatest impediment to liberalism due to its sharply defined doctrines, challenging liberal notions of human perfectibility and the state as our redeemer.

Choosing the Bible as one of the essential reads for conservatives is grounded in the distinction between church and state, rooted in Judeo-Christian differentiation between the supernatural and the natural. This dichotomy safeguards against the state becoming a theocracy or a religion in itself. It's noteworthy that this distinction has been crucial for preventing atrocities in comparison to regimes like Nazi Germany and Soviet Russia.

To clarify, I'm not equating Christianity with conservatism. Conservatives align with religion because it aligns with human nature, encouraging reverence for the past, humility in the face of experiential wisdom, and a justified fear of transgressing moral boundaries encapsulated in "The fear of God is the beginning of wisdom."

Above all, conservatives are realists, acknowledging the existence of original sin. They don't believe government can perfect humanity but are wary that it may become a destructive force fueled by our shortsightedness, unruly passions, foolish schemes, and self-destructive tendencies. While conservatism isn't synonymous with Christianity, conservatives recognize the congruence of central Christian doctrines with humanity's defining characteristics and challenges.

Margaret Thatcher aptly stated that the facts of life are conservative, rooted in our nature. This is precisely why liberals seek to alter human nature, assuming the roles of creator and redeemer. In what it critiques, liberalism reminds us of what we are meant to conserve.

www.ingramcontent.com/pod-product-compliance
Lightning Source LLC
LaVergne TN
LVHW020435080526
838202LV00055B/5207